HARMLESS DREAM OR **URGENT WAKE-UP CALL?**

—⌇〰⌇—

By Rev. Robert F. Legair, M.Div.

xulon
PRESS

Maureen Richards,
May this book be a
blessing to you.

R. Leg

TABLE OF CONTENTS

—◁∿∿▷—

Introduction

—⁓—

I am not an obsessive dreamer. I am certainly not the type of person who eagerly runs to people to tell them about the dreams I occasionally have. To me, dreams are generally a private matter that need not be shared. Even those dreams that seem unusual are not to be shared with just anyone, but with those close to you whom you esteem to be wise and spiritually mature in the Christian faith. However, there was something unique about this particular dream. The vivid images I had seen were not from eating too much pizza the night before, nor were they from watching too many fantasy and science-fiction movies. As much as I like both pizza and the escapism of watching good movies, I cannot attribute the vivid images presented in the dream to either of these things.

The dream I had carried a prophetic message; a message that needed to be shared with as many as possible. God speaks primarily through His Word, but I also believe that He still speaks through dreams today as He has over the past centuries. The important thing about this dream was that its message lined up with the Word of God. In essence, it was fundamentally the same prophetic call to repentance that we see throughout the Bible. I am a firm believer that any dream we receive, even special dreams that we may be able to recollect with striking detail, must never be used to interpret God's Word; rather, God's Word must be used to interpret the dream. This is one of the ways in which we discern whether or not the dream is from the Lord, from our own subconscious imagination, or from a demonic spirit designed to lead us away from the truth.

I ask that before you read any further, please pray that the Lord will help you prepare your heart for what you are about to read and be open to what He is saying to you, not just through this dream, but more importantly, through His Word.

-1-
THE DREAM

In the early morning of August 20, 2006, I had a very unusual dream that I am able to remember in vivid detail, as if I just had it a few moments ago.

The Celestial Highway

I had no idea where I was, but I do recall looking up into the night sky. No moon was in the sky, and I could spot a few stars in the distance, but what caught my attention were what seemed to be shooting stars in the night sky. A good number of them were heading in one direction while a few were heading the opposite way. I thought to myself, "Wow, this is amazing! It's not often that I get the chance to see shooting stars."

At that point I was then given a closer look at these shooting stars to find out that these were not shooting stars at all…they were people. Then it was revealed to me that these were the souls of the deceased who were heading to their eternal destinations. I also could not help but notice that only a small number of these souls were heading upwards while the rest were on their way down. Although they were moving at high speed across the sky, I managed to catch a glimpse of their bodily postures and facial expressions. Those who were heading upward had their bodies in a straight position, arms outspread to the sides or in front of them, heads raised, eyes wide open, and smiles across their faces as if they were eagerly anticipating what was to come. They obviously knew Who would be meeting them on the other side. As for those who were heading downward, they were a different story altogether. Many had bodily postures that were either in a crouched or tucked-in position. Some had a look of fear on their faces while others had an expression of despair and hopelessness. Some even had their eyes closed as if bracing themselves for the horror that awaited them.

A Glimpse into the Underworld

I then found myself in an eerie place. It looked like I was about a mile down a crevice: very eerie and dark with barely a trace of light. Along the crevice walls was a very long set of stairs. I was watching two beings walking down the steps; the much larger one was in front of the other. It was an angel leading a lost soul, a woman, to her chamber. It shortly occurred to me that I was actually witnessing a scene in a part of Hades. Oddly enough, this woman did not seem scared as she followed the angel. I'm not even sure if she realized where she was. Perhaps she felt protected because she was with an angel and thought he would not do anything to harm her. Then again, after seeing how the angel looked, I guess I could understand why she might have felt protected.

This being must have been well over seven feet tall at least, and although he was wearing a bright white robe with a golden belt around his waist, you could still see his massively built frame. He looked very formidable, similar to the angelic being the prophet Daniel saw in a vision he received by the Tigris River (Daniel 10:4-6). On the other hand, the woman he was leading looked like she was covered in black soot from head to toe. I could barely make out if she was even wearing any clothes because of the pitch blackness that covered her body. In Scripture, sin is often associated with darkness. Therefore, the state this woman was in would have depicted the damaging effect sin had on her life.

By the time they reached the door of her chamber, which was large and very exquisitely designed, it slid open to the right (like one of those fancy high-tech sensory doors in Star Trek that would open the moment it detected body heat). When they entered her chamber, what I saw looked quite different from what I expected to see in a place like this. It was nicely posh with modern fixtures, a big screen TV, a stainless steel side-by-side fridge, a fancy high-tech oven, etc. The entire chamber had the appearance of something you would find in the penthouse suite of a five-star hotel. Everything she needed to live sufficiently on her own was there. As she walked in, she said, "Wow! This place is nowhere near as bad as I thought it would be!" She then sat down and used a remote to turn on the big screen TV to watch a show. While all this was happening, I was thinking, "Lord, what *is* happening here?"

Then I found myself outside her quarters watching the angel leave her room. As soon as the door slid shut behind him, the angel transformed into his true demonic state. He retained the same height and massive frame, but he was very dark all over. The only trace of light was in his eyes, which appeared as if they were sunken back into their sockets with dark layers surrounding them. This was a creature you did not want to meet in a dark alley, or any dark place for that matter. Although I was witnessing all of this, I wasn't afraid because I sensed that the Lord was with me as He was showing me this.

The angelic appearance was nothing more than a façade, and the Scripture verse that came to mind was what the apostle Paul wrote, "...For Satan himself transforms into an angel of light"(2 Corinthians 11:14). This demon looked to his right, and in a nearby corner was one of his comrades, another demon, who was standing by a control panel that had buttons and switches on it. As soon as the demon who left the woman's chamber gave a nod to his comrade, the other demon flicked a switch on the panel and a digital timer appeared and counted down five seconds. Once the seconds were up, I was taken back into the room to see what happened next. Apparently, the nicely posh room itself started to dematerialize to unveil the true state of the woman's chamber. Basically, what this poor soul walked into was nothing more than a hologram, an illusion, a lie. She had clearly been deceived.

The place now took on the appearance of the top of an inactive volcano. Most of the floor was covered in lava while brimstone formed the rest of the flooring and walls of what was now her cell. Finally realizing and coming to grips with the deception, the woman ran to where the door was, which was by now a set of thick bars. While grasping the bars, she cried out desperately for the demon to release her. "Let me out! Let me out! You have to let me out of here! Please!"

As she cried out in vain, a fire demon rose up behind her, a creature that looked like a twelve-foot tall wall of fire but with a faceless head, a human-like upper body, and long arms stretched to the sides. This being stood over her as if it was getting ready to envelop her. By that time, I was watching all of this from outside her cell. By the creature's stance, I knew what was going to happen next, so I closed my eyes, turned my head, and walked away. About a couple of seconds later, the next thing I heard were chilling, blood-curdling screams coming from her cell.

The dream, or nightmare at this point, was thankfully over. I did not think I would be able to bear any more of what I was witnessing.

The Interpretation

When I woke up, it was somewhere between 3:00 and 3:30 a.m. I was not able to sleep for a good two hours after that. While I was on my bed trying to make sense of what I just saw, the Lord spoke to me about the dream:

> Robert, there are many out there who are living under the lies and deception of Satan. They are led to believe that they do not need Me in their lives. However, whenever they die without knowing Me and accepting what I did through My Son, Jesus, their eyes are finally opened to what they *would have been delivered from.* Unfortunately, by the time they find out, it will have been too late for them.

-2-
THE AGE-OLD DECEPTION

———ᴧᴧᴧ———

This deception which the Lord spoke of is widely prevalent in our world today. The secular humanistic ideology of ignoring—or worse yet, denying—the stark reality of our sinful condition and our consequent need for God's salvific remedy in our lives has dominated most of our educational systems, especially in the West. These are the very same academic institutions that are shaping the minds of our future leaders. Imagine a generation who:

1. Has absolutely no idea what it means to fear God and no concept of moral absolutes (a basic sense of right or wrong).

2. Does not even recognize God as a living personal being, but instead portrays Him as an abstract theological concept that has been personified by right-winged religious traditionalists.

3. Regards the Bible as an outdated historical book filled with exaggerated stories, abstract statements

which defy human rationale, extreme exclusivism (in reference to Scriptural claims made of Jesus being the *only* way of salvation, thus presenting Christians as narrow-minded elitists), and even hateful literature (due to its uncompromising stance on the homosexual lifestyle).

4. Is taught that the church is irrelevant and is nothing more than a temporary safe haven for the intellectually weak, the marginalized, the persecuted, and the disenfranchised of society.

5. Is convinced that the afterlife is a myth and the very idea of receiving eternal rewards or facing eternal consequences for decisions made in this life is nothing more than a manipulative scare tactic of the Middle Ages.

Then again, after reading the above five points, you may not need to imagine much at all since most of these are already being taught in our school systems and implied in our various forms of media. The bottom line is this: God has not only been marginalized, but He has been completely removed from the picture. Humanistic ideology has taken over the centre stage. Its underlining principles cater to our: need for instant gratification, innately selfish desires and interests, subjective standard of ethics, and unyielding hunger for materialism. Now, it is all about *us* and what *we* want.

The Lie Leading the Blind

Deception is a powerful tool that Satan uses and has used for thousands of years to blind people from seeing the truth. That truth is the blatant reality of their true sinful condition and their need for Christ in their lives. The apostle Paul made reference to this when he wrote to the Christians in Corinth:

"The god of this world has blinded the minds of unbelievers, so that they cannot see the light of the gospel of Christ, who is the image of God" (2 Corinthians 4:4).

Satan's arsenal of weaponry is quite extensive. Nonetheless, of all the deceptive tactics the father of lies has craftily utilized, the philosophy of self-governance is the most subtle yet brutal one of them all. It is subtle in that it does not come across as an obvious deception. In fact, it is often very cleverly disguised in the language of secular humanistic philosophy, where it is presented as the natural sign of psychological progression. According to this kind of thinking, humankind has emerged out of the proverbial cave of ignorance and into the light of reason and science. The idea that our minds have evolved to the point where we no longer need to depend on an all-powerful invisible being for our daily sustenance (let alone our source of salvation) is an appealing thought since we, through scientific discovery, technological advancement, blossoming economic growth, and progressive industrial engineering have learned how to be self-sufficient and independent of any supernatural help. In a way, we have somehow learned how to become our own God, and as a result we no longer see any need for salvation.

Satan has even learned how to disguise this deception with a religious cloak, fooling many in the church to believe that this natural evolutionary course of the human psyche has been divinely ordained by God Himself. This deception in the church would be phrased somewhat like this: "So, like a father patiently teaching his child how to walk on his own two legs, God has been teaching humankind how to be self-dependent instead of running to Him all the time for everything." Though this deception is subtle, it is equally brutal in that it not only robs human beings from the desire to truly become what God has destined them to be, but it simultaneously dooms human-kind to a dreadful eternity that is beyond imagination and without escape.

Jesus made this statement in the gospel of John: "The thief does not come except to steal, and to kill, and to destroy" (John 10:10a). Satan's mandate is to thwart God's plan, and the way he thinks he can do this successfully is to lead us—you and me, the crown of God's creation, His pride and joy—away from Him so we will be separated from Him for all eternity. As Jesus said, Satan's aim is to steal you away from God; to kill and destroy your God-given hopes, dreams, ambitions, and desires. The enemy of our souls, as he is otherwise known, ultimately wants to commit your soul to hell where you would live in agony, being separated from God and loved ones for all eternity. The way he is primarily doing this is through the deception of self-governance, where many are tricked into thinking they do not need God in their lives.

The Thinking of the Carnal Mind—My Way Is Right!

This theme of "my way is the right way!" is a deception that caters to the rebellious instincts in all of us and feeds the gregarious appetites of our sinful nature. The self-gratifying concept of "doing whatever seems right to you" is very attractive. It reeks of rebellion, appealing to that carnal nature in all of us which does not want to come under any order, divine or otherwise. In fact, the only order our carnal nature recognizes and adheres to is its own. The apostle Paul makes mention of this in his letter to the believers in Rome:

> Those who live according to the sinful nature have their minds set on what that nature desires; but those who live in accordance with the Spirit have their minds set on what the Spirit desires...the sinful mind is hostile to God. It does not submit to God's law, nor can it do so. Those controlled by the sinful nature cannot please God.
>
> Romans 8:5-8

By looking at this stark contrast between the mind influenced by the Spirit of God and the mind dominated by the carnal nature, it is easy to see that they are as different as night and day. A person who is governed by the sinful nature cannot please God, because his natural inclination leads him to do the opposite of what God wants him to do. The apostle Paul also writes about this,

> We know that the law is spiritual; but I am unspiritual, sold as a slave to sin. I do not understand what I do. For what I want to do [the right thing] I do not do, but what I hate [the wrong thing], I do... Now if I do what I do not want to do, it is no longer I who do it, but it is sin living in me that does it.
>
> Romans 7:14-15, 20

Here, Paul is saying that due to his sin nature, he is naturally inclined to do what pleases himself as opposed to what pleases God. Sin gives us a false sense of control and freedom to do whatever we want. It also gives us the illusion that everything we do is fine and even pleasing to God. Yet, the author of Proverbs makes the following compelling statement which nicely summarizes the age old deception of self-governance:

> There is a way that seems right to a man, but in the end it leads to death.
>
> Proverbs 14:12

Notice the wording here. The verse did not say that there is a way that *is right* to a man, but a way that *seems right* to a man. If I think of a course of action that I am about to undertake that *seems right* to me, such as taking company-owned office supplies for personal use, or stealing company time, I would not have the confidence to pursue it right away.

If anything, I would first question myself as to whether or not my action would be the right thing to do. After rationalizing my move and determining the lesser evil I would then reach a conclusion: one where my action would be justified. By reasoning out my action, and convincing myself that it is perfectly acceptable, I would have cleared away any doubts or questions I once had in my mind.

A good example of this would be the episode in the Garden of Eden, where Eve was being deceived by the serpent to take the forbidden fruit from the Tree of Knowledge. The first half of Genesis 3:6 gives us an idea of what is going on in Eve's mind while she is being tempted: "So when the woman saw that the tree was good for food, that it was pleasant to the eyes, and a tree desirable to make one wise, she took of its fruit and ate."

The following is what I would imagine how Eve may have organized her thought process:

Questioning Phase: "God did say that we are not to eat any fruit from this tree, but I wonder why? Why this one tree in the garden? What is so special about it? Is He hiding something from us? Can the serpent be right in that God purposely wants to keep the knowledge of good and evil to Himself and keep us in the dark so that we can never be like Him?"

Rationalizing Phase: "The fruit does look delicious and tasty. It would be wrong to allow such fruit to be left alone. If what the serpent said is true, that this fruit can indeed help us know good and evil, then there is no good reason for us to be prohibited from eating the fruit. Perhaps God's instruction for us to stay away is really a test He is doing it to see how much we really want this knowledge. Imagine what it would be like to be just like God! Besides, if He truly did not want us to eat any fruit from this tree, He would never have placed it in this beautiful garden. It makes no sense to leave this fruit alone. Would God really hold back anything good from Adam and me that would enable us to become better? It is not like Him to do that!"

Justifying Phase: "No big deal should be made about what I am about to do, because as far as I am concerned, my motive is right. I am a little hungry, so I need to eat. The fruit looks delicious and should not be wasted. What the serpent told me made sense, and there is nothing wrong with having knowledge of good and evil which this fruit is said to bring me. Besides, if I do get into trouble, I am not the one who really is to blame. It would be the serpent's fault for tricking me. Since he is the instigator behind it, it would only be right for him to take responsibility for what I am about to do. I would be the innocent party in all of this."

Looking at this speculative thought process in Eve's mind, we can see here that by questioning God's instruction as well as rationalizing and justifying what she was about to do, Eve, with the help of the cunning Serpent of course, managed to convince herself that her way was the right way. Adam also willingly complied with the Serpent's advice when Eve offered him the fruit.

The Costly Consequence of a Single Action

Despite God's instruction and warning, both Adam and Eve disobeyed Him, and as a result, death came to humanity. Their eyes were opened, but not the way they had expected. Rather than receiving spiritual and moral enlightenment, they experienced spiritual and moral degradation, as evidenced by their subsequent actions of fleeing from God's presence and refusing to take responsibility for their mistakes. At that crucial moment which decided the fate of all humanity, they felt that eating the fruit from the Tree of Knowledge *seemed* like the right thing to do. They were attracted to the desire for more wisdom, even godhood, but ignored the eternal consequences their actions would have on themselves as well as on their descendants. Both Adam and Eve gave in to the serpent's temptation because they allowed their focus to shift from pleasing God to pleasing themselves. Well, we all know what happened next. Sin entered the world through that single act of disobedience, and as a result, humanity is not only doomed to experience physical death, but spiritual death as well. That blissful connection that Adam and Eve once enjoyed with the Lord was now severed; the relationship humankind once had with God was now gone.

Adam and Eve immediately knew firsthand what the apostle Paul wrote in Romans 6:23a: "For the wages of sin is death." They paid very highly for their sinful act of disobedience, which resulted in their expulsion from paradise (Eden), limited longevity (physical death), and worst of all, a severed relationship with God (spiritual death).

The above example illustrates how the enemy's deception of self-governance (whereby one can seemingly enjoy an endlessly fulfilling life independent of God's help) has been used as effective bait to lure humanity away from recognizing and subsequently fulfilling its divine purpose. What is the divine purpose of humanity? I believe the answer to this question can be summed up in the following Old Testament passage:

Now all has been heard;
here is the conclusion of the matter:
Fear God and keep his commandments,
for this is the whole duty of man.

For God will bring every deed into judgement,
including every hidden thing,
whether it is good or evil.

Ecclesiastes 12:13-14 (*emphasis mine*)

We need to remind ourselves that life itself is a gift given freely to us from God. He created us with the purpose of serving Him and honouring Him with everything He has given us. When we do as the above passage says, our lives will be truly meaningful. When we choose not to do this and decide to pursue a fulfilling life without God, we find ourselves chasing after empty lies disguised as attractions. These attractions fool us into thinking they will be our new source of happiness and even security. As a result, many have pursued a life of fame and fortune, thinking that their fulfillment lied in materialism and riches. However, as many find out (unfortunately too late), a life without God is a life that is truly empty, full of façades—a life well wasted.

A good illustration of this can bee seen in the dream I had in the previous chapter. The moment the woman entered her chamber, she was amazed at what she saw in this lavishly decorated suite. It was in essence fit for a queen and had just about everything she would ever need to enjoy herself comfortably. The electronic equipment was state of the art. From the big screen television to the highly advanced oven, the suite presented the image that the latest technology available was at her fingertips. The modern fixtures and furniture were fashionably designed. These would easily catch the attention of the most meticulous interior designer. Yet, little did she realize that the beautiful room was nothing more than a hologram. What appeared to be a promising afterlife was really a hollow and painful reminder of the deception the woman embraced in her life: a lie that had prevented her from understanding her true purpose (to serve God) and reaching her divine destiny (to be with Him forever).

Proverbs 14:12 illustrates a cunning tactic that the enemy has used for thousands of years, dating as far back as the Garden of Eden. It is the psychological disposition that is highly pervasive in our world today. So much so that it has inadvertently found its way into the church. Like the rest of society, we in the church prefer to do things our way as opposed to God's way. We are so engrossed with ourselves and our way of running God's church, that we will justify our actions as being right in the eyes of God. Like the world, we, too, operate under the delusion that we are fine and that there is nothing wrong with us or with the way we do church ministry. Yet, at the same time, we are unaware of the true state of our soul.

-3-
HAVE WE LEARNED
ANYTHING FROM HISTORY?

—⁓—

Have We Really Learned from the Mistakes of the Monarchs?

The Bible is like a roadmap; it shows us how to get to our destinations. It is the written Word of God, and as such, it is the primary and indispensable means by which God speaks to us. In its pages we receive comfort, assurance, and guidance through the Holy Spirit. Unfortunately, the average Christian does not read the Bible on a daily basis. In fact, a very small percentage of Christians do. If more Christians were to make the time to allow the Word Himself (the *Logos*, Jesus Christ) to speak to them through His written Word, the church in general would be doing much better in its mission. Here is why:

> For the word of God is living and active. Sharper than any double-edged sword, it penetrates even to

dividing soul and spirit, joints and marrow; it judges the thoughts and attitudes of the heart.

Hebrews 4:12

Allowing the Word to judge the attitude of one's hearts helps one to be totally honest with oneself and others, and most of all, to live humbly before God. By receiving a clearer picture of who God is and who he/she is in Christ, the individual has now been given a greater sense of direction and purpose in life. As the Psalmist wrote, "Your word is a lamp to my feet and a light for my path" (Psalm 119:105).

In addition to judging the true intents of one's heart and providing guidance, the Word also gives instruction. This is often done through narratives such as the historical books in the Old Testament, where we learn valuable lessons from the successes and mistakes of others:

For everything that was written in the past was written to teach us, so that through endurance and the encouragement of the Scriptures we might have hope.

Romans 15:4

Therefore, because of these qualities in the word we see that "All Scripture is God-breathed and is useful for teaching, rebuking, correcting, *and training in righteousness*."

2 Timothy 3:16 (*emphasis mine*)

The question I find that we need to ask ourselves is this: have we really learned from what biblical history teaches us? If so, why have we been making the same mistakes over and over and over again? As the old saying goes, "Those who don't learn from history are doomed to repeat it." In light of what Paul wrote in Romans 15:4, mistakes were meant to be learned from, not repeated. I would like for us to look at two monarchs in Israel's past who made costly mistakes. I feel the church today can learn a lot from their example. In fact, I have given them rather unique names to depict the problematic mindset, or should I say the spiritual illness that many in the church are suffering from.

The Saul Syndrome

Now you are probably wondering "what in heaven's name is that?" However, I will explain by painting the context of an incident involving this Old Testament figure and paralleling his mindset with that of many in the church today. Despite his rather disappointing and tragic end, Saul holds the prestigious honour of being the first king of Israel. He became king in a time when judges served as the chief administrators over the tribes of Israel. They already had a king ruling them, God Himself. However, wanting to follow the example of the other nations around them, the Israelites told the prophet Samuel, the chief administrator at the time, that they too wanted a human king to lead them. They were substituting the rule of God for the rule of man (or the rule of a godly king). At this point, the Israelites no longer regarded their unique status as God's chosen people to be a light to the other nations, but instead chose to fit in with everyone else. This, unfortunately, bears a striking resemblance to how Christians today wish to be perceived by the world.

In response to the Israelites' request, a humble Benjamite by the name of Saul from the family of Kish was anointed to be Israel's first king. King Saul started out very well when he commenced his reign as Israel's first monarch. The zeal and reverence he had for God as well as the impressive exploits he did would make you think he was an excellent choice to rule Israel. However, along the way, King Saul started to slip both morally and spiritually. While he and his soldiers were preparing themselves to face the much more formidable

Philistine army at Gilgal, his men were getting nervous. It even got to the point where some of the soldiers were leaving the battle scene. The seventh day came, and still there was no sign of the prophet Samuel who had told him that he would make the sacrifice on that same day. His troops were getting very anxious, and some even crossed back over Jordan to the land of Gilead and Gad (1 Samuel 13:5-7).

Saul felt he needed to do something right away to appease the troops. So instead of exercising his God-given authority as king to order the troops back and to encourage them to wait for Samuel to arrive, he decided to offer up an unauthorized sacrifice to the Lord, something only someone with priestly training like Samuel was qualified to do (vv. 8-10). Saul was no longer honouring the boundaries of his office, and he stepped outside his realm of responsibility when he took on the role of priest. The moment he did, Samuel showed up and gave him a stern rebuke for his disobedience and foolish act of impatience. From that simple act of disobedience and taking matters into his own hands as opposed to relying on God, Saul sealed the fate of his future dynasty (vv. 11-14).

Now the question could be asked, "Why would the future of Saul's throne be threatened by a single act of desperation on his part? Especially since Saul believed he was acting in the best interest of his troops. Doesn't the judgment outweigh the crime?" The judgment may seem drastic from our point of view, but it was necessary.

I believe in order for us to understand the rationale of the judgment, we need to look at the big picture. The judgment pronounced on Saul and his future dynasty had much to do with the highly significant office he held as Israel's monarch. In the book of Genesis, God promised Abram (later known as Abraham) that he would become a great nation and that all the other nations on the earth would be blessed through his descendants (Genesis 12:2-3). Since the Israelites, who are the descendants of Abraham's promised son, Isaac, had been called as God's instrument of blessing to the other nations, it was very crucial for the monarch of Israel to demonstrate complete obedience to God's will.

People tend to emulate the attitudes and actions of those who lead them. If the monarch refused to obey the Lord's instructions, the same attitude would trickle down to the people. As a result, all of Israel would end up turning its back on God, the One who delivered them out of slavery and gave them a new identity. Saul, unfortunately, chose to walk by sight and not by faith in his Creator: a reverse to the way a godly man is called to live according to the apostle Paul (2 Corinthians 5:7).

Another incident occurred in 1 Samuel 15, when King Saul was given a simple yet crucial command from the Lord through the prophet Samuel to completely vanquish the Amalekites. In verse 2 of the same chapter, we are told why such an order was given. According to this verse, the forebears of the Amalekites have ambushed the Israelites when they were in the wilderness. At this point in time, the Israelites were just coming out of four centuries of slavery in Egypt. As newly liberated slaves, the Israelites knew nothing of war. They were not experienced in military combat so they were not at all prepared to engage the Amalekites, or anyone else for that matter, in battle. The Israelites were at their most vulnerable and their enemy knew it. They automatically had the advantage so they seized the moment to attack the Hebrew nomads. Now, centuries later, the time for Amalek's judgment was at hand, and Saul was chosen as the instrument the Lord would use to execute His righteous judgement. However, again, Saul disobeyed what the Lord told him to do. Instead of completely decimating everything they had, not to mention the Amalekites themselves, he instead decided to take Agag, their king, as prisoner. If that was not bad enough, he also took the best of their livestock to be used as a sacrifice to the Lord! Now, I find it outrageous to offer as a sacrifice to God the very thing He told you to destroy. Again, the prophet Samuel gave King Saul the third degree, and rightly so. Saul challenged Samuel's rebuke by insisting that he did execute what the Lord commanded him to do.

> "But I did obey the Lord," Saul said. "I went on the mission the Lord assigned me. I completely destroyed the Amalekites *and brought back Agag their king.*"
> 1 Samuel 15: 20 (*emphasis mine*)

When God said He wanted everyone destroyed, He meant *everyone*, especially the king! This was not a matter of a misunderstanding on King Saul's part. He perfectly understood the nature of his mission, and he knew exactly what he was doing by sparing King Agag's life. Rationalizing, he did what *seemed right* to himself. Because he felt his way was right, he allowed his will to take precedence over God's will.

Furthermore, in the following verse, instead of immediately owning up to his mistakes and repenting to God, Saul, like Adam and Eve, blamed the other person for his actions. In this case, he blamed his soldiers for seizing the best of the livestock as plunder. So now King Saul was not only showing his rebellious attitude to Samuel, but his stubbornness as well. Samuel, in his rebuke to King Saul, equated rebellion (the very heart of the carnal nature) with practicing witchcraft and associated stubbornness with idol worship (1 Samuel 15:23).

Witchcraft is primarily about manipulation and control. It is the dark art that deceives adherents with the delusion that they have more control over their surrounding environment than they think and have the innate power to influence both natural and supernatural forces as they please. Such an ideology puts oneself in the place of God, even making oneself out to *be God* in a sense. Idolatry substitutes the worship of God with the worship of anything else that feeds our sense of gratification. Rebellion, therefore, is very much like witchcraft and idolatry in that it refuses to acknowledge the divine law, order, and authority of God and seeks to establish one's own ways as supreme.

Like King Saul, many in the church have started out very well with the Lord. They have had such a hunger for God in their lives, a devoted prayer life, rigorous Bible study habits, etc. In short, they have had a highly disciplined spiritual walk with the Lord. Unfortunately, the time came where they started to question what they read in the Bible and reason away some of the deep spiritual truths in His Word as being either irrelevant or unrealistic. Before long, they reassume supreme control over their hearts and have relegated God to second place, or hardly any place at all, in their lives. They are now telling God through their actions the reverse of what Jesus prayed in the Garden of Gethsemane: "No longer Thy will, but Mine be done!" Attitudes, behaviours, and actions that were frowned upon in Scripture are embraced and normalized. The biblical teachings of sin, repentance, and holiness are a rarity since they have now been perceived as vague, outdated concepts that are more for the marginalized fundamentalists. They not only justify their current state of lukewarmness as described by the Lord of the Laodicean church in Revelation 3:14-15, they even argue that their current stage of discipleship growth (which is really a state of spiritual complacency) is exactly where God wants them to be. They have now swallowed up the modified version of the deception Proverbs 14:12 warns us about: "There is a way that seems right to a man, but in the end it leads to death." This deception has fooled many in the church with the idea that they have arrived at the summit of their spiritual journey and should be content with where they are.

The Uzziah Complex

As many in the church suffer from the Saul Syndrome, others suffer from the Uzziah Complex, which I believe is even worse. King Uzziah was the name of an Old Testament king of Judah who happened to be one of the longest reigning monarchs in the history of the country (fifty-two years). He started his reign at the age of sixteen and he had a heart that was devoted to God:

> He sought God during the days of Zechariah who instructed him in the fear of the Lord. *As long as he sought the Lord, God gave him success.*
> 2 Chronicles 26:5 (*emphasis mine*)

This should serve as a powerful reminder for all of us, especially those of us who are active in church ministry. Look what happened later on in his rule in verse 16:

> But after Uzziah became powerful, his pride led to his downfall. He was unfaithful to the Lord his God, and entered the temple of the Lord to burn incense.

Does this sound familiar? What is this king doing, assuming the responsibilities of a priest? Uzziah allowed his pride to get the better of him. He went as far as burning incense in the temple, which only the priests were authorized to do. By performing the role of the priest, Uzziah was assuming the role of both priest and king. By doing so, he was assuming that his status was no longer earthly but divine.

God has an established order of who does what in His kingdom, and the moment we attempt to change that order, whether it be out of expediency as in Saul's case or foolish arrogance as in King Uzziah's case, we fall into the danger of usurping God's order for our own sense of order. When Azariah the priest and eighty others confronted King Uzziah in the temple about what he was doing, King Uzziah, who had a censer in his hand, went into a rage before the incense altar (vv. 18-19). Now, of all places to throw a fit, the incense altar was a poor choice. In the temple, the incense altar was not only located in the holy place, but in front of the veil which was the entryway into the Most Holy Place (Holy of holies) where the presence of God was most concentrated. While King Uzziah was raging on the audacity of the priest to challenge his authority, leprosy broke out on his forehead. As a result, he spent the remaining years of his reign in an isolated house.

Saul may have made excuses for his mistakes and even tried to justify them, but Uzziah was so arrogant that he got angry at those who tried to correct him. Pride is the one thing that keeps the church vulnerable and helpless against the enemy's attacks. New Testament Scholar J.T. Hinds writes in his commentary on the book of Revelation, "The unsaved man is more easily aroused to realize his lost condition than the self-satisfied, sleeping Christian who is deceived into thinking himself safe."[1]

Pride blinds us from seeing the truth of who we are and who God is. It causes us to be disillusioned into thinking we do not need God's help, that we can get by just fine on our own. As in the case with King Uzziah, when we are driven by pride, we tend to do foolish things. We exercise poor judgment and our perception of reality is altered.

Many in the church have become susceptible to the enemy's deception because they have been blinded by their pride. As the author of the book of Proverbs wrote, "Pride goes before destruction, and a haughty spirit before a fall" (Proverbs 16:18). Many in the church are heading towards destruction unless they humble themselves before the Lord and repent for taking God's awesome act of grace for granted. Although the destruction I speak of may not necessarily be in reference to their eternal destination (though that in itself is debatable), it is certainly referring to their lives and ministry here on earth.

-4-
ARE WE THE LAODICEAN CHURCH OF THE TWENTY-FIRST CENTURY?

—⌇⌇⌇—

On September 8, nearly three weeks after I had the dream, I was in the Friday evening prayer meeting in my home church. The prayer gathering is normally held in the sanctuary area of our building and usually commences with songs of worship. While a small number of us were singing, I felt this urgency in my heart to go to the front of the church and pray. As I did, the Lord told me to return to where I was sitting and bring the Bible back with me to the altar. When I did that, the Lord instructed me to "Read over the last message I gave to My church in Revelation 3." I turned to Revelation 3 and read the last message Christ gave. It was to the church of Laodicea, which the twenty-first century church seems to mimic. Hear what the Lord tells the apostle John to write:

> I know your deeds, that you are neither cold nor hot. I wish you were either one or the other! So, because

you are lukewarm - neither hot nor cold, I am about
to spit you out of my mouth"
Revelation 3:15-16

" I know your deeds," Notice the Lord never critiqued
them for not doing anything or for not doing enough. Chances
are the Laodicean Church could have been doing a lot in
terms of ministries, programs, etc., but the Lord was well
aware of the motive behind the works, and quite frankly, He
found them distasteful. However, the next thing I read made
me feel like someone had thrust a javelin into my chest:

> Because you say, 'I am rich, have become wealthy,
> and have need of nothing' — and do not know that
> you are wretched, miserable, poor blind and naked —
> I counsel you to buy from Me gold refined in the fire,
> that you may be rich; and white garments, that you
> may be clothed, that the shame of your nakedness
> may not be revealed; and anoint your eyes with eye
> salve, that you may see. As many as I love, I rebuke
> and chasten. Therefore, be zealous and repent.
> Revelation 3:17-19

Now why did the church of Laodicea receive such a
strong rebuke? The key to this question is found in some
background research into the life of the city itself. The
city was located in the region of Asia Minor (present-day
Turkey). A great road ran through the city, which began off
the coast of Ephesus and went as far as inland Asia Minor,
thus making Laodicea a center of trade and commerce.[2] In
addition to the thriving banking industry, a major source of
the city's wealth was the production and sale of its glossy
black wool, which was said to be of very impressive quality.[3]
Laodicea was immensely wealthy. According to Tacitus, a
second century Roman historian, the city showed that it

could cope with anything (even natural disasters like the severe earthquake in A.D. 17) without the aid of any outside help, even imperial help from Rome:

> The same year Laodicea, one of the most famous cities of Asia, having been prostrated by an earthquake, recovered herself by her own resources, and without any relief from us.[4]

The city was not only rich financially, but it was rich in medical resources as well. Laodicea had a famous school of medicine and produced a popular ointment known as Phrygian powder, which was famed as the healing remedy for eye defects.[5] The wealth of Laodicea made its people self-sufficient, so one can imagine how much of this kind of thinking made its way into the church. In such an environment of incredible prosperity, the people, however, had learned to compromise so much that they accommodated the cultural values of their city (perhaps for the sake of tolerance). They never zealously stood for anything, similar to the relativistic mindset our post-modern society has today. As some of my findings indicated, the culture of the city had a profound influence on the Laodicean church, the same way our secular society has impacted the Church today.

The church is oftentimes a mirror image of the city in which it is located. If your church is located in a multicultural community, chances are the make-up of the congregation in your church is bound to be multi-cultural, as mine is. Similarly, the Christians in Laodicea (like the people in its city) were complacent, self-satisfied, and indifferent to real issues of the Christian faith, like discipleship. As a result of such an attitude, the Christians in Laodicea were spiritually blind to their real condition.

The amazing thing I found about Laodicea was that despite its vast wealth, luxurious living, thriving industry, and the celebrity status it had among the cities of Asia, it had a poor water supply.[6] It lacked a supply of drinkable water, the one essential element needed to survive. The water was supplied to the city through pipelines that channelled the water from both the cooler sources in the north and the hotter springs in the south. Since the water traveled through miles of pipeline, it was either cooled down or warmed up, depending on its origin. By the time it finally reached the city, it was neither hot nor cold (like the areas it originated from), but lukewarm due to the change of temperature in the pipelines.[7] When I read about this, I first wondered why Laodicea did not use its vast resources to improve its large-scale plumbing system so that the water's temperature would be kept constant, and thus, more tolerable to drink? I don't know the answer to that question and neither was I able to find an answer. As I pondered about the city's problem with its water supply, the following questions came to me regarding the spiritual condition of its church:

- Could it be that the very manner in which this lavished city treated its water supply (the most essential element for life) was mirrored by the way the church in Laodicea handled its spirituality?
- Could it be that their love for Christ, which at one time was pure, growing, vibrant, and meaningful, had now become diluted, stagnant, apathetic, and meaningless?
- Had their standard for holiness been compromised for the sake of fitting in with their cultural norm?
- Had the Gospel of Christ been modified so that the church could be perceived as more relevant?

Again, the Laodicean church was very much a reflection of its surrounding city. As the city of Laodicea itself lacked the supply of healthy drinkable water, the church also

38

lacked the healthy supply of the Water of Life Himself, who alone can quench humankind's thirst for meaning, purpose, and fulfillment. They, like many prosperous churches today, may have had beautiful buildings, exceptional programs, ministries, musical instruments, and the latest technology, yet they, in their complacency, were missing the most essential element in their church: the Lord Himself. Going back to the words of Jesus that John wrote, "So because you are lukewarm—neither hot nor cold—I am about to spit you out of My mouth." In essence, Jesus was telling this church in Laodicea that, "Since you are so complacent, I find you to be practically useless."

Question: What do you normally do with useless items in your home? You get rid of them. Remember what Jesus said to His disciples when He used the following illustration:

> I am the true vine, and my Father is the gardener. He cuts off every branch in me that bears no fruit, while every branch that does bear fruit he prunes so that it will be even more fruitful.
>
> John 15:1-2

As I read the last few verses, the Lord reminded me of the woman in the dream who was following the angel down the stairway along the crevice wall. I recalled how the woman looked: naked and covered in what looked like black soot all over. Yet while she was following the angel down the steps, she seemed to have paid no heed to how she looked, as if she was completely fine with or oblivious to her state of nakedness and filth. As I also mentioned in the initial account, she seemed to have been undaunted of where she was because of the angel's presence. However, her eyes were blind to the demon's deception. When the woman entered her chambers, she saw that everything she would ever need to live comfortably was right at her fingertips; any aid from an external source did not seem necessary. However, little did she realize that what she walked into was not real at all—it was a lie.

The Lord then said to me that there are many in the church who are just like this woman: spiritually blind to what is around them and unashamed of their nakedness. This is because they have been deceived into thinking that they are in right standing with Him, when they really are not. At this juncture I was reminded of what the Lord told the Laodicean Church through the writings of the apostle John:

> I counsel you to buy from me gold refined in the fire, so you can become rich; and white clothes to wear, so you can cover your shameful nakedness; and salve to put on your eyes, so you can see.
>
> Revelation 3:18

Gold is often a symbol of wealth, power, and influence. Here, Jesus was telling the Laodicean believers to buy the true gold from Himself, gold that had been refined in the fire. Though open to interpretation, gold in this case can signify the real treasures that we all should strive to obtain such as godly character and wisdom. These are the precious jewels that would need time to be refined. They must be tested, developed, strengthened, and honed through the fiery trials we face. It is through the times of tribulation that we truly grow.

Next are the white robes. In this verse, they represent the worthiness of those who were willing to be persecuted to the point of death for their faith. Although white robes have often been associated with holiness and purity, in the book of Revelation they signify worthiness and martyrdom.[8] The following passages make reference to this:

> When he opened the fifth seal, I saw under the altar the souls of those *who had been slain because of the word of God and the testimony they had main-*

tained. They called out in a loud voice, "How long, Sovereign Lord, holy and true, until you judge the inhabitants of the earth and avenge our blood?" *Then each of them was given a white robe*, and they were told to wait a little longer, until the number of their fellow servants and brothers who were to be killed as they had been was completed.

Revelation 6:9-11 (emphasis mine)

After this I looked and there before me was a great multitude that no one could count, from every nation, tribe, people and language, standing before the throne and in front of the Lamb. *They were wearing white robes* and were holding palm branches in their hands...Then one of the elders asked me, "These in white robes – who are they, and where did they come from?" I answered, "Sir, you know." And he said, *"These are they who have come out of the great Tribulation*; they have washed their robes and made them white in the blood of the Lamb.

Revelation 7:9-14 (emphasis mine)

This plea for the Laodiceans to wear white robes to cover their nakedness implies that the believers in that city were not ready to make the radical choice to suffer for their faith. The very same question could be asked of us today: Are we willing to suffer or even die for our faith? If you are honest with yourself and you find yourself thinking twice, this may be an indicator of how you prioritize your life. Does the Lord and His kingdom truly have top priority in your life, or do you find your own self-interest taking precedence over everything and everyone else, including the Lord? If you find that God does not have top priority in your life, you are not alone. Countless of other Christians, including myself, would have answered the above questions in a similar way. As a result of being spiritually clueless and blind, many in the church are living under the delusion that they have enough intelligence, ingenuity and technology to live their lives without His help. Again, the powerfully convincing deception of self-governance has long made its way into the church.

I was then reminded of the first part of the dream with the shooting stars. Again, I could not help but remember that the majority of them were heading downward. Then the Lord said to me that there were many in the church who were simply not ready for His return, nor were they ready to meet Him because they had never repented of their sins. At that moment I broke down and cried my heart out, lying prostrate before the Lord. I knew in my heart that this message was not only for my local church, it was for the universal Church, for believers everywhere who would fall in the category of their "lukewarm" Laodicean forebears.

-5-
SOUND THE ALARM! AWAKE THE SLEEPING GIANT!

—⁓—

It Is Time to Wake Up!

Now the question could be asked, "How did the church reach to this state of complacency? How is it that Christians have become indifferent to the matters of faith and discipleship? I believe the answer could be found in a story of the lifesaving station that has been powerfully and eloquently presented by the late University of Chicago theologian, Langdon Gilkey:

> On a dangerous seacoast where shipwrecks often occur there was once a crude little lifesaving station. The building was just a hut, and there was only one boat, but the few devoted members kept a constant watch over the sea, and with no thought of themselves went out day and night tirelessly searching for the lost. Many lives were saved by this wonderful little station, so that it became famous. Some of those who

were saved, and various others in the surrounding area, wanted to become associated with the station and give of their time and money and effort for the support of the work. New boats were bought and new crews trained. The little lifesaving station grew.

Some of the members of the lifesaving station were unhappy that the building was so crude and poorly equipped. They felt that a more comfortable place should be provided as the first refuge of those saved from the sea. So they replaced the emergency cots with beds and put better furniture in the enlarged building. Now the lifesaving station became a popular gathering place for its members, and they decorated it beautifully and furnished it exquisitely, because they used it as a sort of club. Fewer members were now interested in going out to sea on lifesaving missions, so they hired lifeboat crews to do this work. The lifesaving motif still prevailed in the club's decorations, and there was a liturgical lifeboat in the room where the club initiations were held. About this time a large ship was wrecked off the coast, and the hired crews brought in boatloads of cold, wet, and half-drowned people. They were dirty and sick, and some of them had black skin, and some had yellow skin. The beautiful new club was in chaos. So the property committee immediately had the shower house built outside the club where victims of shipwreck could be cleaned up before coming inside.

At the next meeting, there was a split in the club membership. Most of the members wanted to stop the club's lifesaving activities as being unpleasant and a hindrance to the normal social life of the club. Some members insisted upon lifesaving as their primary purpose and pointed out that they were still called a lifesaving station. But they were finally voted down and were told that if they wanted to save the lives of all the various kinds of people who were shipwrecked in those waters, they could begin their own lifesaving station down the coast. They did. As the years went by, the new station experienced the same changes that have occurred in the old. It evolved into a club, and yet another lifesaving station was founded. History continued to repeat itself, and if you visit the sea coast today, you will find a number of exclusive clubs along that shore. Shipwrecks were frequent in those waters, but most of the people drown.[9]

As depicted in this vivid analogy, many Christians have lost sight of their divine purpose. Rather than becoming mature disciples of Christ with a clear focus in mind to influence and lead the lost to Christ, many believers choose instead to be complacent and focused on themselves. The color of the sanctuary carpet takes precedence over developing new strategies in reaching out to the lost in their communities and providing discipleship training to help them become all that God wants them to be. In this state of complacency, many in the church have diverted their focus from what is really important (executing the Great Commission) to the minor things which really do not matter in the grand scheme of things. Personal wants, interests, and agendas slowly take centre stage while the affairs of God and His kingdom get pushed out into the periphery. Like the people of the lifesaving station, bringing Christ to the lost is no longer a priority. In fact, it seems as if the Great Commission has now been perceived as the Great Suggestion. Many Christians feel that this command is not for them; that it is more for those who are professionally trained to do evangelistic ministry.

Question: Are we all not commanded by Christ to share the Good News about Jesus? If we profess to be followers of Christ who share the Father's love for sinners everywhere, should we not also share the Father's love and compassion for the lost? While we remain so preoccupied with who has the largest building, the best choir, the most members, the longest history, the latest technology, the best music, the most programs, etc., have we lost sight of our original purpose as the church? Have we somehow fallen asleep so that we have become clueless and unaware of what is happening around us?

It is time for the church, especially in the Western culture, to awaken from its slumber and be aware of its true state. Many Christians are living their lives under the deception that everything is well with them, when it is not. Many in the church are so far removed from God that they no longer know what it means to fear the Lord or to live a life of holiness. They do not understand the serious consequences sin has in one's life and, therefore, hardly see the need for repentance. They feel that since God is a God of love and mercy, He will readily pardon or even overlook the sin they secretly practice in their lives. After all, we are living under grace right? However, that is just the problem. We tend to take this word, *grace*, very lightly and I believe it is because many of us do not really understand what grace really means.

True Grace Is Not Cheap

More often than not, the word *grace* that is typically referred to by the twenty-first century church is really the cheap grace that German theologian and martyr Dietrich Bonhoeffer writes about in *The Cost of Discipleship*:

> Grace without price; grace without cost! The essence of grace, we suppose, is that the account has been paid in advance; and, because it has been paid, everything

can be had for nothing. Since the cost was infinite, the possibilities of using and spending it are infinite. What would grace be if it were not cheap?...Cheap grace means the justification of sin without the justification of the sinner. Grace alone does everything, they say, and so everything can remain as it was before...Well then, let the Christian live like the rest of the world, let him model himself on the world's standards in every sphere of life, and not presumptuously aspire to live a different life under grace from his old life under sin....Cheap grace is not the kind of forgiveness of sin which frees us from the toils of sin. Cheap grace is the grace we bestow on ourselves. Cheap grace is the preaching of forgiveness without requiring repentance, baptism without church discipline, communion without confession, absolution without personal confession. Cheap grace is grace without discipleship, grace without the cross, grace without Jesus Christ, living and incarnate. ...This cheap grace has been no less disastrous to our own spiritual lives. Instead of opening up the way to Christ it has closed it. Instead of calling us to follow Christ, it has hardened us to our disobedience...Deceived and weakened, men felt that they were strong now that they were in possession of this cheap grace – whereas they had in fact lost the power to live the life of discipleship and obedience. The word of cheap grace has been the ruin of more Christians than any commandment of works.[10]

So what is grace? In a nutshell, grace is unmerited favour. The word *grace* is derived from the Greek word *charis*, which signifies favour, goodwill, or lovingkindness granted by a superior to an inferior. It is not something that can be earned or deserved; rather, it is a gracious gift. As the apostle

Paul writes to the Ephesian church, "For by grace you are saved through faith; and not of yourselves: it is the gift of God: not of works, lest any man should boast" (Ephesians 2:8-10).

Although Scripture is flooded with examples of God's grace towards humanity, the best example of the redemptive quality of God's grace can be found in Paul's epistle to the believers in Rome:

> You see, at just the right time, when we were still powerless, Christ died for the ungodly. Very rarely will anyone die for a righteous man, though for a good man someone might possibly dare to die. But God demonstrates his own love for us in this: While we were still sinners, Christ died for us.
>
> Romans 5:6-8

Grace that has been given to us at such a high price, the very life of Christ Himself, should not be taken for granted nor esteemed lightly. Grace should certainly not be seen as permission for Christians to continue living their life in sin. The grace of God requires change in a sinner's conduct or character. Dr. John Hagee, senior pastor of the Cornerstone Church in San Antonio, Texas, once made this statement in his sermon on grace: "Forgiveness granted to anyone without demanding a change in character makes the grace of God an accomplice to evil."[11]

I strongly agree with this statement and would also add that grace is not a license to sin; rather, it provides an opportunity for change. A good example of this could be found in John 8:1-11, when Jesus rescued a woman who was caught in the act of adultery by the Pharisees and experts in the Jewish law. After He dispersed the angry mob, He asked the woman where her persecutors were. She looked around and saw no one except Jesus standing there with her. Jesus then told her, "Neither do I condemn you. Go and sin no more" (John 8:11). In essence, Jesus was saying this, "I just spared you from the death penalty which, according to the Mosaic law, you rightly deserved. However, I have given you a second chance. Go in My grace and change your ways. If you choose to continue in your life of sin, something much worse will happen to you."

In a way, Jesus gave the Laodicean Church a similar warning when He told them He would spit them out of His mouth unless they changed from their lukewarm state of complacency (much like the state many in the church are in today). It was important for the Laodicean church to receive this harsh wake-up call because over three centuries later, in 363 A.D., the city itself would play a very important role in church history. It was at this time that the Council in Laodicea, comprised of thirty clerics, would come together to select books that would fit the criteria of canonized literature. These very books make up the holy bible Protestant churches use everywhere. Therefore, in playing such a vital role in the formation of the Holy Writ, it was important for the Laodicean church in the first century to be awakened to their true state in the eyes of the Lord.

In reading over the first three chapters of Revelation, I found it interesting that of the seven churches the Lord had the apostle John write to, five of them (Ephesus, Pergamos, Thyatira, Sardis, and Laodicea) were told to repent. If you do the math, more than seventy-one percent of the believers John was writing to were told to repent! The last commandment the Lord gave the church was not necessarily the Great Commission, but for us to repent.

-6-
THE UNIVERSAL CALL TO REPENT

—*wws*—

The Meaning of Repentance

So, what does it really mean to repent? Repentance is not simply telling God you are sorry. Rather, it is a heartfelt sorrow for sin that leads to the renouncing of it, a sincere commitment to forsake it, and walking in obedience to Christ.[12]

Repentance involves three things:

1. Your Intellect: It all begins with you acknowledging the sin in your life and understanding that it is wrong. You can rationalize and justify your actions all you want, but regardless of how you look at it, sin is sin and it is not something any believer should ignore, let alone tolerate.

2. Your Emotions: Emotionally, you approve what the Bible teaches about sin. Sometimes the facts we know intellectually do not concur with our feelings emotionally. For example, we *know* that smoking is bad for our health. We are aware of what smoking does to the lungs as well as the other destructive results of its addiction, which shortens a person's longevity. Yet those who smoke will tell you of the irresistible craving they have for some nicotine. Although they are aware of the health hazard of smoking, they still feel that it can satisfy their momentary discomfort. The same could be said for any type of addiction. By allowing the scriptural truth of sin to impact you emotionally (not just intellectually), you then will find yourself having a deep remorse for the sin or a godly sorrow towards it, as the apostle Paul calls it in 2 Corinthians 7:10. This, in turn, leads us to have a hatred of it. We find the sin repulsive, we detest it, and we want absolutely nothing to do with it.

3. Your Will: Once you acknowledge the sin in your life and detest it for its true hideousness, you will then be motivated to act. Here is where the will comes in. By exercising your will, you are making a personal decision to turn from the sin, renounce it, forsake it, and lead a life of obedience to Christ instead. Notice that there are two things happening here: you are *turning away* from the sin and *turning towards* Christ in faith. It is not possible to have a successful, growing, victorious Christian life if one is done without the other. If you simply just turn away from sin without turning to Christ, who will give you the strength you need to overcome your temptations? You will find your-

self fighting a losing battle, because rather than relying on God's grace to see you through those moments of temptation, you are solely relying on your will to resist them. Remember, you are no match for the enemy alone, but with Christ, you are more than a conqueror. Vice versa. If you were to turn to Christ without renouncing and turning away from the sin in your life, your walk with the Lord would be a constant struggle and you would start to wonder why you had not experienced a change in life that you heard others talk about in their lives. You would not know what it means to be free in Christ because you would have never experienced that same freedom for yourself. The sinful nature would still dominate your life. I like the way Bob Krajcik puts it: "Remorse sees the bitter end of sin, repentance (*metanoew*) breaks free from it."[13] You have truly repented when you have completed the last step with your will by renouncing the sin, forsaking it, and turning to Christ in faith.

As Wayne Grudem aptly puts it,

Repentance occurs in the heart and involves the whole person in a decision to turn from sin. Merely having sorrow for one's actions, even deep remorse, does not constitute genuine repentance unless it is accompanied by a sincere decision to forsake sin that is being committed against God.[14]

Many of us wonder why we're not getting the breakthrough we need, and it is all because we have never really repented of the sins in our lives. Many Christians are under the impression that simply saying to God, "I'm sorry, and I won't do it again" is enough. Yet little do they realize that unless they purposely resolve in their hearts to renounce and forsake the sin they have committed against God, sin will always be the cause for their frustration, discouragement, fear, ungodly behaviour, and even demonic bondage. Any hidden sin that has not been exposed will be used as a foothold for the enemy of our souls. Simply going to the altar and pouring out tears of regret to the point where you form little puddles of teardrops will not do a thing for you unless you make the sincere commitment to forsake the sin in your life. Some Christians seem to think that the more emotional you are, the more motivated the Lord will be to respond in your favour. This type of childlike manipulation may work with some parents, but it certainly will not work with God. Unless you genuinely repent of your sins, all your hollering, crying, weeping, and wailing will not move God to do anything anymore than a howling wind will move a mountain.

Sin Needs to Be Exposed

Unless the sin in our lives is exposed through our verbal confession and renunciation, it will always be there to stunt our spiritual growth and be a deadly snare to us as believers in Christ. Let us not forget about the sin of Achan.

The following narrative can be found in Joshua 7. Shortly after Joshua led the Israelites to a successful mission of bringing down the nearly invincible city of Jericho (with the Lord's help, of course), spies were sent to investigate the neighbouring city of Ai, which was much less formidable. They reported back to Joshua that only a few thousand men were needed to overtake the city, which was deemed an easy win in comparison to Jericho. However, though Ai was significantly smaller and less powerful, the people of Ai shamefully defeated the Israelites. Bewildered and frustrated, Joshua cried to God, and the Lord answered Joshua by telling him about the sin Israel committed in His sight. The Lord reminded Joshua about the command He had him give the Israelites before they laid siege to Jericho—that no man was to take any detestable thing from among the people of Jericho except the silver, gold, and vessels of bronze and iron, which were to be brought into the treasury of the Lord (Joshua 6:18-19). The Lord then pointed out to Joshua that one of the Israelites disobeyed the command, and as a result caused Israel to experience an embarrassing defeat by the people of Ai. Joshua was then instructed by God to destroy the one responsible so that Israel would once again be in right standing with God.

After an investigation, Joshua found out that Achan, through his own confession, was the one responsible. Achan admitted that the spoils he took looked very appealing to him (the same way sin gratifies the carnal nature), so he desired to keep them, even if it meant breaking the Lord's command. By taking the accursed objects, Achan became accursed himself, and as a result he and his family were given the death penalty by stoning. Achan was no evil lowlife; he was a member in the faith community of Israel. In fact, he came from the royal tribe of Judah that was destined to be the tribe from which some of the greatest monarchs in Israel's history would emerge, like David, Solomon, Uzziah, and the Messiah Himself. However, regardless of his lineage, he was susceptible to the greed in his heart which made him embrace the very things God called accursed. He fell prey to the same temptation that the serpent gave Eve, so you can imagine that the similar *speculative* thought process mentioned earlier may have gone on in Achan's mind.

This demonstrates that our deeds impact not only ourselves, but those around us as well. Because of Achan's sin, Israel suffered disgrace at the hands of a weaker enemy, and his own family had to suffer the consequences for his selfish actions. From this example, we Christians should wisely take heed of what Joshua told the Israelites shortly after the Lord revealed to him the cause of their failed mission to Ai:

> Sanctify yourselves for tomorrow, because thus says the Lord God of Israel: "There is an accursed thing in your midst, O Israel; *you cannot stand before your enemies until you take away the accursed thing from among you.*"
>
> Joshua 7:13 (emphasis mine)

The "accursed thing" (which can signify unconfessed sin) cannot be put away from us unless we repent. If we do not repent of our sins, we will not be able to stand against the devil and his cunning schemes. By our not repenting of our sins, this begs the question of whether or not many of us who profess to be Christians are even saved. Our lifestyles are really no different from those of the unsaved. We talk the same way (i.e. through the use of inappropriate language and lying), behave the same way, and even dress the same way.

Just as an aside, I am not saying that Christians should look old-fashioned, or that women should wear Victorian-style dresses from the nineteenth century and men should bring back the '50s look. There are plenty of trendy clothing styles out there that will do justice to various body types, and make you look like a million dollars, but when you dress in a way that is sexually provocative or in a way that would make you look like you just got out of bed or would lead anyone to easily identify you as a possible member of a street gang, then you may have crossed the line a bit. I strongly believe that who you are in the inside will be reflected on the outside. True, clothes do not make the man or woman, but they do say a lot about you. If you are a believer and you may have taken issue with what I have just said, before you crucify me, ask yourself this question: "Who am I really representing whenever I am walking in any public place?" If we profess to be children of the King and joint-heirs with Christ, let us at least look the part. Now I understand I may have opened a can of worms with this hotly debated topic, so I will just move along quickly and leave that between you and the Lord.

Regardless of how attractive the life of sin may appear with its temporary pleasures (which are not really pleasant at all if you really think about it), sin in general is very ugly. Yes, human beings have been created in the image of God, but due to their sinful nature, that image has been disfigured and marred. Because of this natural human condition, we look nothing like our Creator in terms of our actions, speech, thinking, and attitude. Thanks to sin, we have become the misshapen form of what we were supposed to be. A good illustration of this would be the disturbing image in my dream of the woman's condition. Her entire body being covered in dark soot made her look rather unsightly. The darkness that covered her body was so intense that she was virtually pitch black! She looked nothing at all like the woman her Creator intended her to be. It was because of her sinful life that she appeared the way she did. In life, she may have worn the most elegant and expensive dresses, put on the most fancy make-up, and presented the image of one who was not only gorgeously attractive, but who was living large. Yet, the sin in her life had damaged her mentally, emotionally, and spiritually. It had eaten away every aspect of her true inner beauty until she inevitably looked like nothing more than a dark shadow from the abyss with a human outline. She may have even done a great deal for charity and done a lot of other good deeds in her life. However, regardless of how numerous her noble acts of kindness were, they have done absolutely nothing to help her sinful condition. As the prophet Isaiah writes, "All of us have become like one who is unclean, and all our righteous acts are like filthy rags; we all shrivel up like a leaf, and like the wind our sins sweep us away" (Isaiah

64:6). This woman in the dream reminded me of the destructive side effect sin has on all of us.

Sin Can Be Conquered

Now, I am not saying that we are to be perfect because that is impossible. I also understand that human beings are by nature sinful, and even when a person accepts Christ as Lord of their lives, that does not mean the sinful nature will be completely eradicated from their life. Nevertheless, as a believer, you are no longer under the dominating power of sin because you have been liberated from its bondage. You are now free to live the way God intended you to live. The reason I feel it is necessary to make this point is that some Christians feel that since we are not completely free from sin's influence in our lives, it is pointless to fight it daily (to be transformed by the renewing of our minds — Romans 12:2a) and to live a life of holiness. Naturally, it would be discouraging, to say the least, if we were left to contend with the sinful nature on our own. We would be fighting a losing battle. However, one crucial thing we must remember is that the sinful nature can be conquered, and this can only be made possible through the power of the Holy Spirit. It is only through the redemptive work of the Son and the sanctifying work of the Holy Spirit that it is possible for us to have a relationship with the Father.

However, having a relationship with God does not mean that we no longer contend with sin at all. Let us look at an example from the book of Genesis at the beginning of the Old Testament, where Cain is in dialogue with the Lord. Hear what the Lord tells Cain when He addresses him about an unacceptable sacrifice:

If you do what is right, will you not be accepted? But
if you do not do well, *sin is crouching* at your door; it
desires to have you, *but you must master it.*

Genesis 4:7 (*emphasis mine*)

Now remember, the Lord was not talking to an immoral
person who had no idea who He was. He and Cain had a relationship; although it likely was not as good as the fellowship
the Lord had with Cain's younger brother, Abel. Scripture
shows that Cain did have a relationship with God, as
evidenced by the dialogue between them in Genesis 4:1-15.
Yet, the Lord told Cain that if he did not do what is right, i.e.,
present his sacrifice with the right heart, sin was crouching
at the door. God did not say that sin was ruling his heart,
otherwise He and Cain would not have any relationship, but
He described the sin in Cain's life as something that was
eagerly looking for an opportunity to take over. The Lord
told Cain that he must master the sin in his life or it would
take control. God would never have told Cain to do this if it
was not possible for him to do so. Similarly, many Christians
seem to follow Cain's example. They have the same attitude
as he did, whenever they drop their tithe or offering into the
offering plate, or engage in any type of church ministry with
a miserable, sour attitude. Christians have been set free from
the power of sin, but they, like both Cain and Achan, allow
the sin nature to influence them. As a result, they too end up
making poor choices in their lives that keep themselves spiritually immobilized, preventing them from moving forward
or operating at the spiritual level they ought to be. The enemy
has even fooled many Christians into thinking that they have
not been truly set free from sin's dominion, because of the
presence of sin in their lives. But, let us not forget what Paul
wrote to the believers in Rome concerning this,

Since we have been united with him in his death, we will also be raised to life as he was. We know that our old sinful selves were crucified with Christ so that sin might lose its power in our lives. We are no longer slaves to sin. For when we died with Christ we were set free from the power of sin... So you also should consider yourselves to be dead to the power of sin and alive to God through Christ Jesus. Do not let sin control the way you live; do not give in to sinful desires. Do not let any part of your body become an instrument of evil to serve sin. Instead, give yourselves completely to God, for you were dead, but now you have new life. So use your whole body as an instrument to do what is right for the glory of God. Sin is no longer your master, for you no longer live under the requirements of the law. Instead, you live under the freedom of God's grace.

Romans 6:5-7, 11-14

The apostle Paul wrote that we should be dead to the power of sin, but what does that mean? Perhaps this example will help: Do you know of anyone who is a deep sleeper? Maybe you are one yourself. Such a person can sleep through pretty much anything. If you were to get two large drum cymbals and bring them together to make a loud sound, it would not move someone who is in deep sleep. Even a 6.0 Richter-scale earthquake would not wake them. People who sleep like this are completely oblivious to their surroundings; they are literally dead to the world.

This is what we believers need to be to the sinful nature. Sin is enticing, attractive, and alluring, but since believers have symbolically died with Christ and buried the old nature, sin should no longer have any influence in their life. This, of course, does not mean that believers are no longer able to make any mistakes or have reached perfection. The only time we will be completely rid of the sinful nature is when either one of two events takes place in our lives: 1) Christ returns and we are transformed into our glorified state of perfection, or 2) through death we leave this earth to enter God's presence.

So for the time being, as long as we are living in this fallen world we have to contend with the sinful nature. However, as believers who have been set free from sin's domineering power, we could chose not to sin. We do not have to be lead astray by various temptations or fall prey to any sort of addiction. We could resist the urge to gossip or to engage in slanderous conversations, dirty language, and lying. Remember, since we are dead to sin, we are now made alive in Christ. Since we have awakened or have been resurrected to a new life in Christ, we have a strong desire to live for Christ. As we grow in Christ, we engage more in behaviour that is motivated by a growing love for others. People are the centre of God's heart, and we increasingly share His affection for people, especially for the lost. We will be motivated to lead a life of submission to God as Jesus did.

Being made alive in Christ also means that the Spirit of Christ influences a great degree of our actions as well as the way we think. Rather than being fearful of what the next day will bring or having our minds plagued by Murphy's Law, we can allow "the peace of God to rule our hearts" (Colossians 3:15a). I would just like to expound on this point for a moment. Although Christians have been saved from the punishment of sin, liberated through the redemptive work of Christ on the cross, and given eternal hope through His resurrection, many of them cannot say they are at peace in their hearts. They still retain their sinful habits, and as a result, they live with the guilt the enemy uses to taunt them. As a result, they are unable to experience the peace of God. As far as they are concerned, they are still under condemnation. However, let us not forget what Paul wrote to the believers in Rome:

There is therefore now no condemnation to those
who are in Christ Jesus, *who do not walk according
to the flesh, but according to the Spirit.*
Romans 8:1 (*emphasis mine*)

Yes, Christ paid the ultimate price for our sins with His
very own life; therefore, we are no longer under the condemnation of the law. However, the decision is still up to us to
decide whether or not we wish to forsake the sin in our lives
and turn to Christ, believing that He will meet *all* of our
needs. Whenever we doubt that the Lord can meet a certain
need in our lives and we turn back into the sinful practice
that helped us to cope or get by before, we are bringing down
upon ourselves the condemnation of the law.

As the apostle indicates, there is nothing wrong with the
Mosaic law itself; in fact, it is there to instruct us on how to
live right in the sight of God. However, no matter how good
a person is, no one can live according to the righteous standards of the law without the help of God. We simply cannot
live the Christian life on our own. We need God's help every
step of the way. The moment we get the idea of indicating to
God that "we can take over from here," we are inadvertently
saying to God that "our way is best." Sound familiar? This
deception of self-governance and pride needs to be crucified
in our hearts and minds while we clothe ourselves with that
Christ-like humility that says, "Not my will but Yours be
done."

Being dead to the old sinful nature brings about other
changes whereby we become less judgmental and more
loving, less negative and more positive, less fearful and more
bold, less attracted to sin and more attracted to holiness, less
inclined to follow the carnal nature and more inclined to
follow the spiritual nature, and ultimately less like ourselves
and more like Christ. This last point does not mean that we
lose our God-given sense of identity; rather, it simply means

that as we become more like our Creator, His image in us (that has been marred by sin) is being restored. The more it is restored in us, the more you and I become what were meant to be. So, in a way, by losing one's self in Christ, one actually finds themselves. Though we would still be unique in our individuality, we simultaneously would be the mirrored reflection of His holiness and perfection.

Repentance Is the Key to Revival and Restoration

When we genuinely repent of our sins, we experience the refreshingly liberating work of the Spirit. We are released from spiritual bondages that have prevented us from becoming all God destined us to be as His children. Many are aware of the current state the church is in, and therefore see the need for God to do "a new thing" amongst His people. That is why there is an outcry for revival and restoration and even deliverance to sweep across our countries. However, this will not happen unless the church heeds the Lord's call to repent. What the Lord told Solomon could very well be the prophetic word for our church today:

> If My people who are called by My Name will humble themselves and pray, seek My face *and turn from their wicked ways*, then will I hear from heaven, and will forgive their sins and heal their land.
> 2 Chronicles 7:14 (*emphasis mine*)

Many of us who desire for God to bring about revival may humble ourselves, pray fervently, and seek the face of God, but we still fall short because we did not turn ourselves away from things that were displeasing to Him. We tend to do the first three steps, but either miss or ignore the last and perhaps most essential one.

A Lesson from Nineveh

The church today can learn a lot from the example of the Ninevites. You may recall the story of Jonah. He was called by the Lord to deliver a message to the citizens of Nineveh and refused to do so because of their notorious reputation. Jonah obviously did not share the same compassion for them the Lord did. He was not at all willing to give the people of that city a second chance. In fact, he wanted them to be destroyed for their indescribable wickedness. He felt these people were incorrigible, beyond help, and even out of reach for divine redemption, so he fled in the opposite direction to Tarshish (most Old Testament scholars believe that this city was located in southern Spain).

Shortly afterwards, God sent a storm to unnerve the crew and even used their superstitious beliefs to point to Jonah as the cause of their problems, which Jonah himself admitted. Once they threw him off the ship, the sea calmed down and the Lord sent Shamu's big brother to take Jonah on an express ride to Nineveh. At that point, Jonah was forced to rethink his options; either obey God's directive, or take a little trip down the whale's digestive tract.

Once the whale arrived off the south western coast of Mesopotamia, he vomited Jonah out. Jonah then headed to the city and delivered a message of warning to the citizens of Nineveh: "Forty more days and Nineveh will be overturned" (Jonah 3:4b). The notorious citizens of Nineveh reacted quite differently to Jonah's message than he anticipated:

> The Ninevites believed God. They declared a fast, and all of them, from the greatest to the least, put on sackcloth.

> When the news reached the king of Nineveh, he rose from his throne, took off his royal robes, covered himself with sackcloth and sat down in the dust.

Then he issued a proclamation in Nineveh:

"By the decree of the king and his nobles:
Do not let any man or beast, herd or flock, taste anything; do not let them eat or drink. But let man and beast be covered with sackcloth. Let everyone call urgently on God. Let them give up their evil ways and their violence. Who knows? God may yet relent and with compassion turn from his fierce anger so we will not perish..."

When God saw what they did, and how they turned from their evil ways, he had compassion and did not bring upon them the destruction he had threatened.

Jonah 3:5-10

Notice how the Ninevites reacted to Jonah's message. They *all* repented, from the least to the greatest. I have found the reaction of the king of Nineveh to be very impressive. He put aside his royal robe which signified his power, authority, influence, and social status and wore sackcloth (a shirt composed of a rough cloth made from goat hair) and made a public edict commanding all citizens of the city to fast. Such an act of humility moved the heart of God, so the Lord withheld raining His judgment upon the city.

Now, if a wicked city like Nineveh could be spared from God's judgement by simply repenting, what do you think will happen if the church today were to do the same? God said that if we, His people, not only humble ourselves, pray, seek His face, but also turn from our wicked ways (in other words, repent), then we will see an incredible outbreak of God's power like never before. By fulfilling the last essential requirement—repentance—the Lord will hear our prayers, forgive our sins, and heal our land through revival and restoration.

We also need to follow King David's example in allowing the Spirit of God to show us with His light of truth the areas in our hearts where we may be harbouring some hidden sins that need to be confessed:

Search me, O God, and know my heart; test me and know my anxious thoughts. See if there is any offensive way in me, and lead me in the way everlasting.

Psalm 139:23-24

Notice how David is asking the Lord to do this searching for him, because he himself is not fully aware of what lies deep within his subconscious. As the Old Testament prophet Jeremiah writes, "The heart is deceitful above all things and desperately wicked. Who can know it?" (Jeremiah 17:9)

Knowing this truth about the human heart, David understood that he was not qualified to be his own judge. He needed the Lord Himself, the unbiased, impartial, righteous Judge to do this deep internal searching for him. He probably felt that if this type of searching was left up to him, he would not find anything wrong with himself and would easily overlook or justify some questionable thinking and attitudes in his heart. We need to do this very same thing in our own lives so that we can properly fulfill the divine mandate that Christ has given to the church.

If you feel that the Lord has really spoken to you or challenged you as you are nearing the end of this book, I invite you to put the book aside and read over what the Psalmist wrote in Psalm 139:23-24, which I quoted earlier. Make that your own prayer. Afterwards, allow anywhere from two to five minutes of silently waiting on the Lord to show you anything offensive in your own heart, anything which you would need to repent. Once that thing (could be an unconfessed sin in your life) has been exposed to you, read Psalm 51:1-13. This particular psalm was also written by David, but, according to Old Testament scholars, it was a prayer of repentance he wrote after the prophet Nathan helped him come to grips with his crime against Uriah and his sin against God. The passage reads as follows:

> Have mercy on me, O God,
> according to your unfailing love;
> according to your great compassion
> blot out my transgressions.
>
> Wash away all my iniquity
> and cleanse me from my sin.
>
> For I know my transgressions,
> and my sin is always before me.
>
> Against you, you only, have I sinned
> and don what is evil in your sight,
> so that you are proved right when you speak
> and justified when you judge.
>
> Surely I was sinful at birth,
> sinful from the time my mother conceived me.
>
> Surely you desire truth in the inner parts;
> you teach me wisdom in the inmost place.
>
> Cleanse me with hyssop and I will be clean;
> wash me and I will be whiter than snow.
>
> Let me hear joy and gladness;
> let the bones you have crushed rejoice.
>
> Hide your face from my sins
> and blot out all my iniquity.

Create in me a pure heart, O God,
and renew a steadfast spirit within me.

Do not cast me from your presence
or take your Holy Spirit from me.

Restore to me the joy of your salvation
and grant me a willing spirit to sustain me.

Then I will teach transgressors your ways,
and sinners will turn back to you.

Psalm 51:1-13

Repentance Leads Us To Fulfill Our Purpose

It is through repentance that the joy of His salvation is restored to us. When this happens, we, the church, will effectively fulfill our mandate of making disciples. When we make disciples, we are doing what Jesus commissioned us in Matthew 28:20, "teaching them to observe all that I commanded you" (NKJV). So to reiterate what David wrote in Psalm 51:13, we teach transgressors the ways of God by teaching them to observe *everything* Christ has commanded us. It is about time for the days of Cafeteria Christianity — where we only select elements of our faith that we find appealing and ignore other areas that we find uncomfortable — to be finally over.

If we Christians are to become all that God has destined us to be, we must apply *all* of Christ's teachings to every area of our lives, especially the two greatest commands that still serve as the paramount pillars of our faith: 1. Love the Lord your God with all your heart, soul, and mind; 2. Love your neighbour as yourself. When we genuinely love God with the entirety of our being, we have little difficulty doing what He says. Likewise, when we truly love our neighbours as ourselves, we won't hesitate for a moment to share with them the good news of the hope found only in Christ.

To effectively reach out to communities, our generation, our world, we must stay connected to the source Himself. So what does it mean to stay connected to God? Does it mean to simply pray more, study the Bible more, fast more, etc.? As commendable as all these spiritual disciplines are, we must not lose sight of the crucially important element of a growing relationship with the Lord. After Jesus gave a sharp rebuke to the Laodicean church for their lukewarmness and self-sufficience, He reminded them in Revelation 3:19 that He chastises those whom He loves. Those strong words of correction telling them to shape up were really words that said, "Listen, I care about you too much to allow you to remain in the state that you are in now! You need to change!"

Hear what He says in the following verse: "Behold I stand at the door and knock. If anyone hears my voice and opens the door, I will come in to him *and dine with him* and *he with Me*" (Revelation 3:20). This verse has often been used to make reference to Jesus knocking on the door of the hearts of sinners, but in context, Jesus was actually speaking to believers. These were believers who had been complacent with their spiritual condition because they had been deceived into thinking that their material prosperity was a sign of the Lord's favour on their lives. They allowed their external "blessings" or possessions to determine their status in God's eyes. They failed to realize that the Lord was far more interested in the state of their hearts.

The church was a reflection of their city; just as water, the most essential element for life, was not a priority to the city of Laodicea, the Water of Life, Jesus Christ Himself, was not a priority to the believers. It seemed as if the Lord's position shifted from being the Lord of their hearts to the Lord standing on the outside of their hearts, knocking and waiting to be invited inside again. This tends to happen when we get a little too comfortable and complacent. We feel we have enough to get by. The Lord has done His part, and we feel as if we can take over where He left off and operate the ship without Him. The Lord is then left on the outside looking in, while we assume the place of supreme authority over our lives.

The deception of self-governance fuels our pride and arrogance as we ascend once again to the throne of our hearts, not realizing that we are unwittingly setting ourselves up for a terrible fall. The Lord has every right to walk away and leave us to our eventual downfall and ultimate destruction, yet instead, He chooses to remain at the door and knock. Revelation 3:20 does not indicate nor imply a set limit of the number of times the Lord would knock (i.e., after the third time, He would then leave us to our fate). He instead waits and waits, ever patiently until we, like the prodigal son, finally come to our senses and realize the extent of our folly. When we rush to answer His knocking, to our relief, He is right there waiting for us to invite Him in and to take His rightful place as Lord of our lives.

-7-
LET'S TALK...OVER LUNCH

—⁓—

Come, Let Us Dine Together!

Something special happens when we open the door of our hearts to let the Saviour in. Not only does He reign as Lord of our lives, but He also wishes to dine with us, to share in our meal. Let us take a closer look at what the Lord says in the second half of verse 20: "I will come in to him and dine with him..."

We begin to understand how Zaccheus must have felt when Jesus offered to stay by his home. Zaccheus was the notorious tax collector who was ostracized from his fellow Jews and labelled a traitor for working for the Roman government. I could only imagine how surprised and humbled he must have felt when Jesus chose him, of all people, as His very own special dinner guest. We, too, experience both a tremendous sense of honour as well as a sense of unworthiness that the King who we blindly mistreated would offer to share a meal with us. More is happening here in the heart than Jesus simply having a meal with you and I. Mealtime, especially in the Jewish culture, provided the opportunity for fellowship in the form of discussion, debates, sharing and learning (not only from each other, but also from the Torah). Mealtime also provided the opportunity for participants to engage in reflection, worship, and prayer. The dinner table was a place of bonding.

We, in the Western culture, experience a similar type of bonding whenever we share a table with others. If you're sitting at the same table with someone you don't know, eating together will provide the opportunity for the two of you to get know each other better by way of conversation. As time progresses, you may realize and even be shocked by how much the two of you have in common. You get to know more about that person, and as your knowledge of them grows, you will feel more comfortable being with them. By the time the meal is over, you might have exchanged phone numbers, email addresses, or even business cards because you are looking forward to getting connected again with that person in the future. A wonderful friendship has emerged simply by having a meal together.

This is what happens when our Lord comes into our hearts and dines with us. He is willing to eat what we eat. Even if what we have to offer is not much, nor proper for someone of His calibre, He does not smirk, roll His eyes, have a look of disgust or hesitation, or complain. Rather, He gladly shares in our dining experience. The more He shows His willingness to meet us where we are at, the more our trust for Him grows and the more we feel comfortable around Him. We wish to learn from Him and we increasingly antici-pate our mealtimes together with Him as He shares with us more and more of who He is. Verse 20 of Revelation 3, as you may know, does not end here, but it continues: "...and he with Me."

If I were to tell you I am having dinner with someone, it is usually implied that I have been invited to a mealtime engagement by the other party. Likewise, as we have seen earlier, when Jesus said that "I will come and dine with him…" this tells me the Lord has been willing to meet us where we are at the moment we invite Him into our heart. He does not bulldoze Himself to the throne of our hearts. Rather, He gently comes along and walks besides us in our journey as we try to make sense of life, the same way He did with the two disciples who were walking along the Emmaus Road in Luke 24:13-28. He proves Himself to be Emmanuel (God with us) by listening to us and by simply being there for us. He graciously joins us for the meal that we have prepared so that He can have a taste of our own little world. As the Lord came down to humanity's level two thousand years ago, He likewise will also meet us individually at our own level, regardless of our stage in life. The way we prepare our meals is a strong indicator of how we see our world, understand life, make sense of our purpose here on earth; how we truly perceive ourselves, others and the Lord Himself .

In time, our relationship reaches the point where we allow Him to take the lead in preparing our meals. We watch Him as He shows us step by step how to make one that is truly fit for a king. He leads us to move out of our comfort zone, a familiar way of doing things, into the unknown, which takes meal preparation to a completely different level. We then begin to see our world from His perspective and gain a deeper understanding of who He is, who we are and our purpose in life. Since we are out of our element, we dare not do things His way without His help. Little by little, day by day, we are given a new glimpse of who this Master Chef is, and we anticipate not only having dinner with Him at the table, but tasting the fine cuisines that are prepared by Him. Since He has been invited to take the lead in our hearts, He invites us to the table to share in the meal He has prepared for us. As your relationship with Him grows, He then shares with you the significant event in the not-too-distant future, the incredibly wonderful occasion you eagerly anticipate. That glorious moment is the

Marriage Supper, a feast unlike anything you have ever experienced, one that will be of cosmic proportions. He also tells you that you will be His honoured guest and that He has a spot specially reserved for you. No one will start the dinner until you are there. You are then given greater insight into how special and worthwhile you really are. Before you know it, a wonderful, close, and lasting friendship has emerged simple by having a meal together. This would not have been possible if you had not first responded to His knocking and invited Him into your heart.

> In My Father's house are many mansions; if it were not so, I would have told you. I go to prepare a place for you. And if I go to prepare a place for you, I will come again and receive you to Myself; that where I am, there you may be also.
>
> John 14:2-3

We see in this analogy of "dining at the table" how the transitions have been made from the Lord joining us in our journey, to coming alongside to be with us, and finally being invited to take the lead. In each of these transitions, the heart of the person changes continually to become more and more open to the Lord's work. The level of trust will have reached the point where we can say to the Lord, "Okay, I've tried it my way all this time, but I'm slowly starting to realize that my way is not the right way. You take the lead, and I will follow You. Show me how it should be done and help me to apply it so that it will come to me naturally. I want Your way to be like second nature to me because Your way is best. Not my will, Lord, but Yours be done!"

Before you know it, a radical transformation has taken place in both your heart as well as your mind. Your very thinking has been changed. The dining experience with the Lord often leads to life-changing moments, very special moments you will not experience elsewhere or through anyone else. As the Catholic theologian Fr. Joseph G. Donders aptly puts it,

> Things happened when people ate with Jesus. Bread and fish were multiplied, water turned into wine, sins were forgiven, feet washed, hope revived, and new perspectives in life were opened up.[15]

-8-
JUST A HARMLESS DREAM OR AN URGENT WAKE-UP CALL?

———

There are many ways in which God speaks to us. He primarily does this through His Word, the Bible, but He also uses sermons, music, and numerous other ways. He is not limited in the manner in which He reaches out to us. However, as He has done in biblical times, God also speaks powerfully through visions and dreams. I will not go into depth about the differences between a vision and a dream. I once read somewhere that the main difference between the two is that visions occur while you are awake while dreams happen when you sleep. Regardless of what the differences are, I believe that both are still effective means by which God gets His messages across.

As I mentioned in the introduction of this book, I am not much of a big dreamer. Even the *unusual* dreams I have had I keep to myself unless I see the need to share them with someone who is spiritually wise and mature in the faith. This dream, however, is unlike any that I have had before, and I felt the Spirit prompting me to share this dream with you because it is far more than just a dream.

There is a prophetic message here that needs to be heard; first, by the church, and second, by the world. In reflecting back on the content of the dream, I first thought it was a message only for those who do not know Christ. However, over time, the Lord showed me this was essentially for His church and that it had a dual purpose: to wake up many believers from their spiritual slumber, and to get them to take a serious inventory of their own lives. This is very much needed, especially in our day and age. We do not want to end up like the five foolish virgins in one of Jesus' parables (Matthew 25:1-13) who allowed the oil in their lamps to run out and thus were not prepared for their bridegroom's arrival. As a result, instead of meeting the bridegroom, they were shut out from the celebration. Contrary to what I have been taught before, the five foolish virgins do not represent the unsaved sinners, but the complacent members of the church who felt they knew best how to handle God's program. Sound familiar? Let us not forget what Peter writes,

> For it is time for judgment to begin with the family of God; and if it begins with us, what will the outcome be *for those who do not obey the gospel of God?* And, "if it is hard for the righteous to be saved, what will become of the ungodly and the sinner?" So then, those who suffer according to God's will should commit themselves to their *faithful* Creator and continue to do good.
>
> 1 Peter 4:17-19

Notice Peter did not say "those who are *ignorant* of the gospel of God," but "those who *do not obey* the gospel of God." He is speaking of those who have a knowledge of the gospel but are simply being disobedient to what it says. Also, notice the distinction between the ungodly and the sinner; he was not talking about the same group of people, but two different camps who will apparently suffer the same fate. The ungodly are those who know God, come to church, sing in the choir, do all other sorts of religious stuff, but have no fear of God. These people do as they please. Sinners, on the other hand, want nothing to do with God. Which camp do you find yourself in, the camp of the righteous or the ungodly? The foolish virgins would represent the latter.

The Lord wants His people to be aware of the age-old deception the enemy has used to rob many of their blessings and to hold even more in bondage. He wants us to understand the mistakes the Israelite monarchs (like Saul and Uzziah) made and to *learn* from them rather than repeat them. He does not want us to be lukewarm in our spirituality like the first century Laodicean church, but to be the loving, wise, vibrant body of royal priests He has called us to be. He wants us to be aware of the present spiritual state of the church and what it needs to do in order for it to effectively and successfully accomplish what it has been mandated to do.

Speaking of the mandate of the church, this leads us to the second purpose of this message, which is to remind us of our responsibility of being His witnesses to this lost, dark world. There is a very unpleasant afterlife awaiting those who do not know Christ, one that is very real. Yes, being a child of God is an awesome privilege, but this awesome privilege comes with an awesome responsibility. We will one day be held accountable for what we did with our testimony and how we lived out our faith. There is a world out there that is hungry and desperately searching for the truth about life, themselves and God. You, who not only know the truth but have *the* truth in your heart, should not keep silent. Let others know so they, too, can be set free from the relentlessly unyielding power of sin.

Those of you who may not have grown up with any church background, who are still searching for *the* right way, or perhaps are even sceptical about what you have just read, may be asking yourself the question that is similar to the very title of this book: Is all this really nothing more than a harmless dream? Or is there a powerful message behind all of this calling us to wake-up to the reality of the eternal destinations that await us on the other side of death?

I understand that some of you may rationalize that the dream I described at the beginning of the book was nothing more than the playing out of images from the subconscious level of my mind, images that had been shaped by my personal religious convictions. I think not! We in this post-modern age tend to ignore or explain away things we do not understand or are unable to empirically prove by way of scientific experimentation. Nonetheless, friends, hell is a very real place. It is not a medieval fabrication conjured up by zealous monks and priests to scare the illiterate, ignorant, and gullible into going to church. It is very much biblical. If you do a thorough study of Jesus' earthly ministry, you will see that He spoke more about hell than He did about heaven. In fact, He went as far as offering up His very own life as the ultimate sacrifice so that we would not have to end up in that place.

As I was writing this, the horrid scene at the end of my dream came to my mind, when the woman realized she had fallen for the same lie (of security and fulfillment outside of Christ) in death as she did in life. I noticed that when she cried out for help, she did not call out to God to save her, but to the demon guard to release her from her prison. Perhaps she knew that, at this point, her fate was sealed and divine judgment had already been rendered; therefore, there was no way for God to respond to her cry for mercy. I remember vividly how the faceless demonic creature engulfed in flames stood over her. It was ready to cover her in its blaze. At that moment, I thought to myself, "My God, there is absolutely no way for her to escape! She is doomed for all eternity!" As I turned away and heard the chilling screams coming from her cell, fear gripped me like never before. I also experienced a tremendous sense of pity for the woman, knowing that her screams would not reduce the intensity of her pain, nor would her cries for help be acknowledged by God anymore. At that point, she was beyond help. I could not even begin to imagine the pain she was experiencing, having her entire body swallowed up in flames.

Have you ever burned your finger or your hand in an accident? Do you remember how much pain you felt from that incident? Try imagining your entire body engulfed in flames. The pain you had in your mishap would be multiplied a million times, to say the least. I am not sure if *all* the lost souls suffer the same type of physical torment, but I do believe that the emotional and mental anguish they feel would be quite unbearable. The agony would be greatly intensified as they were reminded of the numerous opportunities they had in life to turn their lives to Christ, opportunities they had ignored and neglected. If that is not bad enough, there will come a time when they will participate in what is called the Second Resurrection, or the Resurrection of the Unjust. Here, the unrighteous dead will rise from their graves and will be brought before the Great White Throne to receive a formal sentencing into the lake of fire (Revelation 20:11-15). I would imagine the lake of fire being even worse than the fire in Hades, because Hades itself would be thrown into this unblessed inferno.

Think about this for a moment: the human spirit, like any other spirit, is immortal. No spirit can ever be destroyed or annihilated even by the fire of the Second Death. There will never come a time when the human spirit will no longer exist. This means that the lost souls will be tormented by the flames *forever!* However, the most troubling thing about hell is not even the torment the lost souls are forced to endure, but its permanence. Once you are in, there is no way of getting out!

Now many have asked the question, why would a loving God send anyone to a place like hell? The truth is God has never sent a single soul to this horrid place. You send yourself there by rejecting the gospel and refusing to acknowledge the gracious work of redemption that the Lord Jesus did for you on the cross. God has blessed humanity with the gift of freewill: with it, we can choose whether or not to serve Him. God does not want to force anyone to serve Him. He respects our decision, and this alone can be another reason why hell exists apart from being made for the devil and his angels (Matthew 25:41). As omnipotent as God is, He will never interfere with our freewill. If people choose not to have God as part of their lives, then a place is reserved for them to live out that existence for all eternity. What is that place called? You guessed it...hell.

However, the good news about hell is that you do not have to go there! The Lord has provided a way of escape from an unimaginable eternity of total separation from loved ones (family and friends) and most of all, from Himself. In doing so, He has given a wonderful opportunity for us to experience the incredibly fulfilling rewards of eternal life through His Son, Jesus Christ.

Jesus said to him, "I am the way, the truth, and the life.
No one comes to the Father except through Me."
John 14:6

Eternal life is the richly meaningful relationship with the Lord that can be experienced in this life and maximized to the fullest in the hereafter. The Lord desires for you to be with Him for all eternity, which is why He did what He had to do.

For God so loved the world that He gave His only begotten Son, that whoever believes in Him will not perish, but have eternal life.

John 3:16

This blissful existence with God is the exact opposite of hell. Think of the most wonderful, breathtaking experience you ever had on this earth. Imagine that being multiplied a billion times (this is just a conservative estimate). That is the type of eternity God wants for you. He wants you to live in close proximity to Him so He can continually reveal to you a greater facet of His glory and the unending depth of His power and love. He wants *you* to live, walk, learn, laugh, rest, and *be* in His presence forever. Heaven is very much everything that hell is not, everything life in this present world can never be. In his letter to the Corinthian church, the apostle Paul quoted the following statement from Scripture,

No eye has seen, no ear has heard, nor mind has conceived what God has prepared for those who love Him.

1 Corinthians 2:9

If you have never made a personal commitment to follow Christ and receive eternal life, will you respond to the Lord's *gracious* invitation today?

Come to Me, all you who labour and are heavy laden, and I will give you rest.

Matthew 11:28

The following is a sample of the salvation prayer. You are more than welcome to use it as your own as long as you mean it from your heart or put it into your own words as long as your prayer has the following elements to it:

1. Acknowledgement/admittance that you are a sinner.
2. Recognition of what Jesus Christ did for you (Rom. 10:8-10). He died on the cross and rose from the dead on the third day.
3. Asking the Lord to forgive you of your sins.
4. Asking Him to come into your life and be Lord of your life.

Dear Heavenly Father,

Thank You for loving me and for Your wonderful grace that You have shown in my life. Thank You for sending Your Son, Jesus Christ, to die on the cross for my sins. Father, I admit that I am a sinner and, therefore, humbly ask that You forgive me for all of my sins and cleanse me from all unrighteousness.

Lord Jesus, thank You for dying for me and for giving me hope through Your resurrection, both in this life and in the blessed afterlife. I ask You, Lord Jesus, to come into my heart and be Lord of my life. By the power of Your Spirit, help me to become the person You have intended me to be, and lead me away from the path of destruction.

Thank You, dear Lord, for hearing my prayer as I repent of my sins and turn my life over to You. In the Name of Your Son Jesus Christ,

Amen.

Did you pray
the salvation prayer to invite the
Lord into your heart?

—〜〜—

Please tell us about your experience:

The Humberlea Church of God
6807 Steeles Ave. W.
Etobicoke, ON
M9V 4R9
Telephone: (416) 743-5861
Email: humberlea@hotmail.com

End Notes

———~~~———

1. John T. Hinds, *Revelation: A Commentary on the Book of Revelation*, 1989 (Nashville: Gospel Advocate Company), 62.

2. Kenneth L. Barker and John R. Kohlenberger III, *NIV Bible Commentary. Volume 2, New Testament*, 1994 (Grand Rapids: Zondervan Publishing House), 1152.

3. Ibid.

4. Tacitus, *The Annals by Publius Cornelius Tacitus, Book 14* (A.D. 59-62), 14:27.

5. Kenneth L. Barker and John R. Kohlenberger III, *NIV Bible Commentary. Volume 2, New Testament*, 1994 (Grand Rapids: Zondervan Publishing House), 1153.

6. Ibid.

7. Ibid.

8. Dr. Ian A. Fair, "Laodicea," *The Center for Church Enrichment*, <http://www.centerce.org/BIBL666/Laodicea.htm>.

9. Langdon Gilkey, How the Church Can Minister to the World Without Losing It (New York: Harper & Rowe 1951).

10. Dietrich Bonhoeffer, *The Cost of Discipleship* (London: SCM Press Ltd.), 35-36.

11. John Hagee, *The Dispensation of Grace. Revelation of Truth Vol. 9.*

12. Wayne Grudem, *Systematic Theology* (Grand Rapids: Zondervan Publishing House), 713.

13. Bob Krajcik, *Bible Study Letters Online Tracts— Repentance: What Does the Word Mean?* 4.

14. Wayne Grudem, *Systematic Theology* (London: InterVarsity Press), 713.

15. Fr. Joseph G. Donders, *The Word Among Us: Being at the Table With Jesus*, <http://www.wau.org/current/article.asp.html>.

References

—⁓—

Barker, Kenneth L., and Kohlenberger III, John R. *NIV Bible Commentary. Volume 2, New Testament.* Grand Rapids: Zondervan Publishing House, 1994.

Bonhoeffer, Dietrich. *The Cost of Discipleship.* London: SCM Press, 2001.

Donders, Fr. Joseph G. "Being at the Table with Jesus," *The Word Among Us*, 23 August 2006, <http://www.wau.org/current/article.asp.html>.

Fair, Dr. Ian A. "Laodicea," *The Center for Church Enrichment*, 23 August 2006, <http://www.centerec.org/BIBL666/Laodicea.htm>.

Gilkey, Langdon. *How the Church Can Minister to the World Without Losing It.* New York: Harper & Rowe, 1951.

Grudem, Wayne. *Systematic Theology.* Grand Rapids: Zondervan Publishing House, 1995.

Hagee, John. *The Dispensation of Grace. The Revelation of Truth Vol. 9.*

Hinds, John T. *Revelation: A Commentary on the Book of Revelation.* Nashville: Gospel Advocate Company, 1989.

Krajcik, Bob. "Repentance: What does The Word Mean?" *Bible Study Letters Online Tracts*, 23 August 2006, <hhtp://www.bright.net./~bkrajcik/repentdefine. htm>.

Tacitus, Publius. *The Annals of Publius Cornelius Tacitus.* Book 14 A.D. 59-62.

Printed in the United States
81335LV00002B/328-525